SCHIRMER'S LIBRARY
OF MUSICAL CLASSICS

Vol. 203

EDVARD GRIEG

Op. 46

First Orchestra Suite

From the Music to
"PEER GYNT"

(Dramatic Poem by H. Ibsen)

Adapted for Concert Performance and
Arranged for Piano, Four-Hands by
THE COMPOSER

Edited and Fingered by
LOUIS OESTERLE

ISBN 978-0-7935-5222-1

G. SCHIRMER, Inc.

DISTRIBUTED BY

HAL•LEONARD®
CORPORATION
7777 W. BLUEMOUND RD. P.O. BOX 13819 MILWAUKEE, WI 53213

Contents.

14653

Morgenstimmung.
(Morning-mood.)

Edited and fingered by
Louis Oesterle.

Secondo.

EDVARD GRIEG. Op. 46, No 1.

Allegretto pastorale. (♩. = 60)

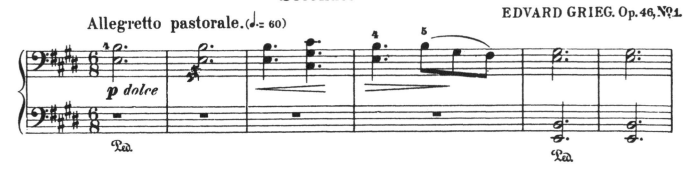

Morgenstimmung.
(Morning-mood.)

Primo.

Edited and fingered by
Louis Oesterle.

Allegretto pastorale. (♩.=60)

EDVARD GRIEG. Op.46, № 1.

14658 r×

Secondo.

Secondo.

Ases Tod.
(Ase's Death.)

Edited and fingerd by
Louis Oesterle.

Andante doloroso. (♩=50) **Secondo.**

EDVARD GRIEG. Op. 46, No 2.

Åses Tod.
(Ase's Death.)

Edited and fingered by
Louis Oesterle.

Primo.

EDVARD GRIEG. Op. 46, Nº 2.

Andante doloroso. (♩ = 50.)

14653

Anitras Tanz.
(Dance of Anitra.)

Edited and fingered by
Louis Oesterle.

Secondo.

EDVARD GRIEG. Op. 46, No. 3.

Tempo di Mazurka. (♩ = 160.)

14653

Anitras Tanz.
(Dance of Anitra.)

Edited and fingered by
Louis Oesterle.

Tempo di Mazurka. (♩ = 160.) **Primo.** EDVARD GRIEG. Op. 46, № 3.

+) Trills without after-beat.

14653

In der Halle des Bergkönigs.
(In the Hall of the Mountain-king.)
Secondo.

Edited and fingered by
Louis Oesterle.

EDVARD GRIEG. Op. 46, No 4.

Alla marcia e molto marcato. (♩=138.)

pp staccato sempre

A

B

p

poco a poco cresc.

In der Halle des Bergkönigs.
(In the Hall of the Mountain-king.)

Primo.

Edited and fingered by
Louis Oesterle.

EDVARD GRIEG. Op.46, № 4.

Alla marcia e molto marcato. (♩=138.)

Secondo.

Secondo.